FOR ORGANS, PIANOS & ELECTRONIC KEYBOARDS

E-Z PLAY® TODAY

176

THE CHARLIE BROWN COLLECTION™

CONTENTS

T0045096

ISBN 978-0-634-03167-0

HAL•LEONARD®
CORPORATION

7777 W. BLUEMOUND RD. P.O. BOX 13819 MILWAUKEE, WI 53213

Visit Hal Leonard Online at
www.halleonard.com

Baseball Theme

Registration 8
Rhythm: Waltz

By Vince Guaraldi

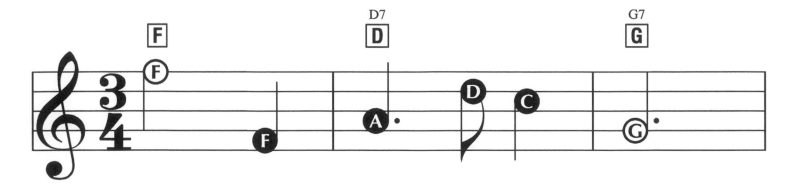

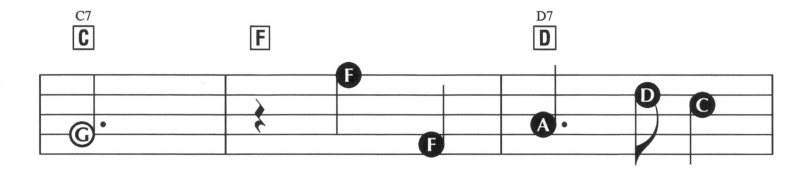

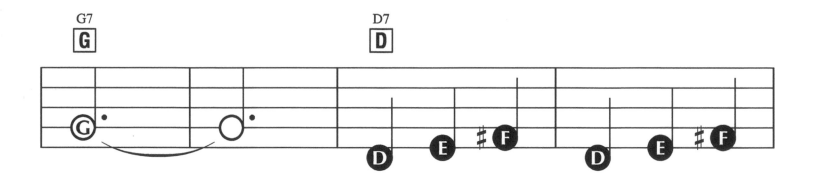

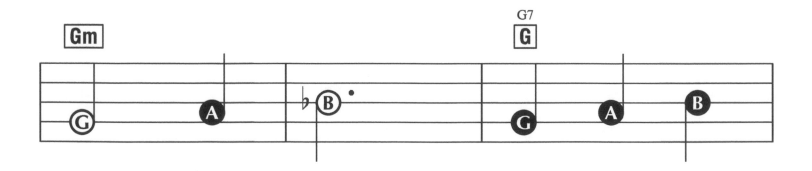

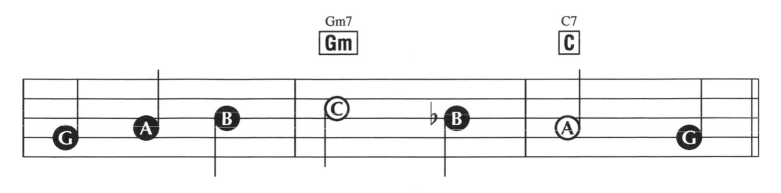

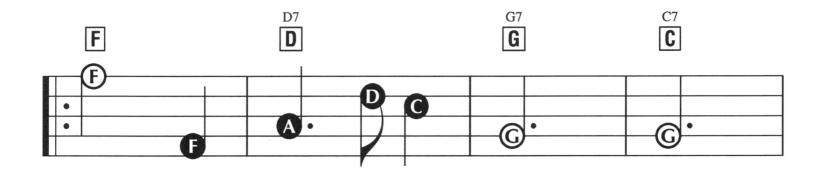

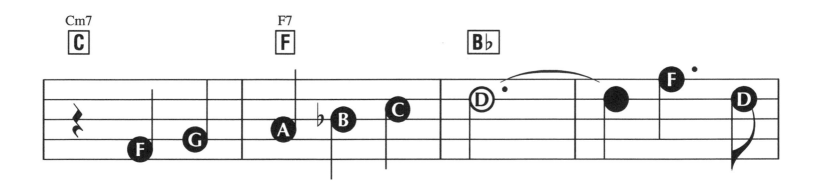

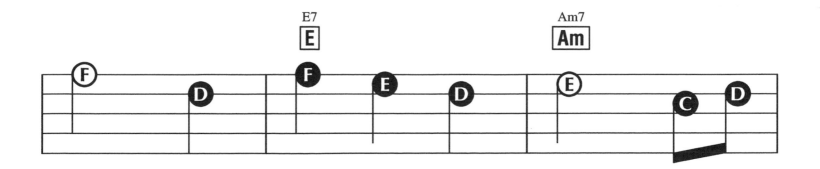

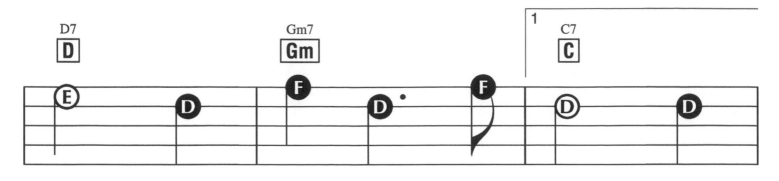

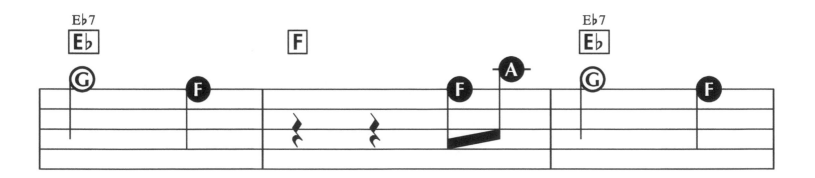

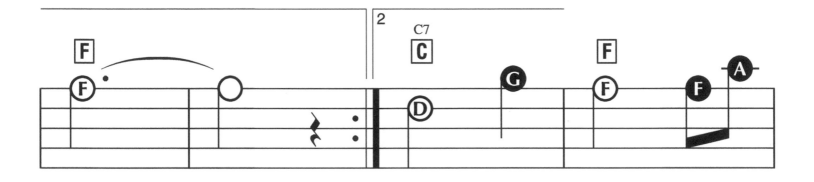

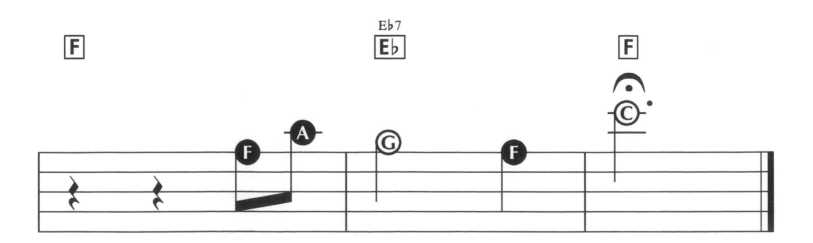

Charlie Brown Theme

Registration 8
Rhythm: Big Band or Swing

By Vince Guaraldi

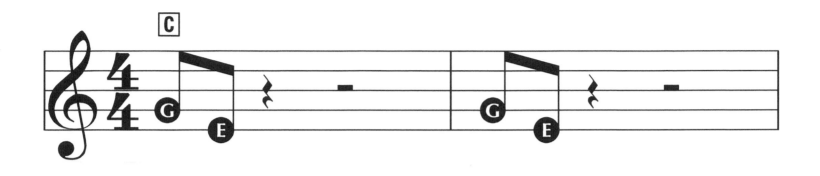

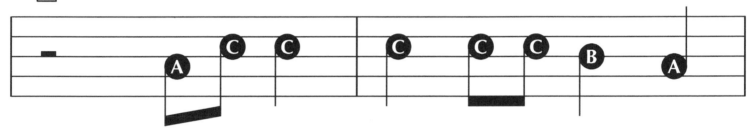

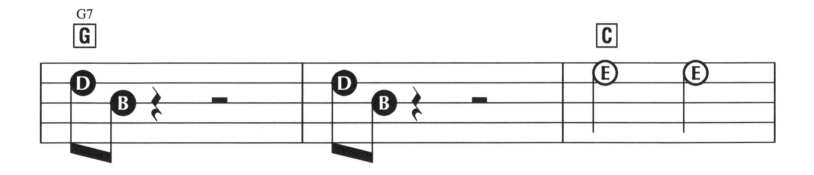

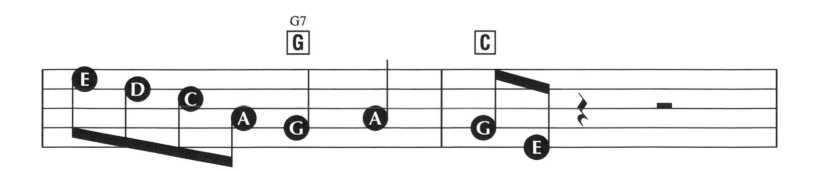

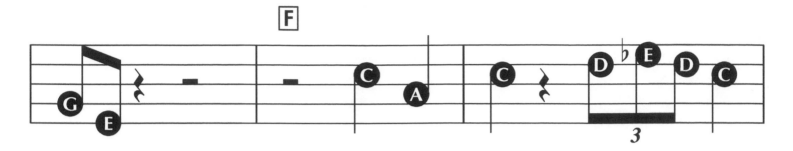

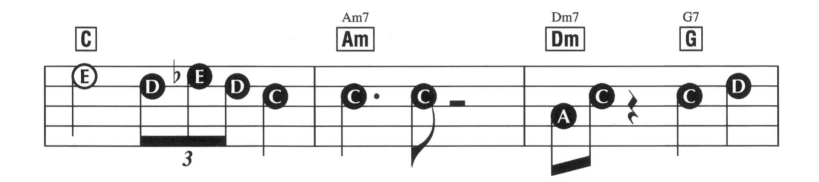

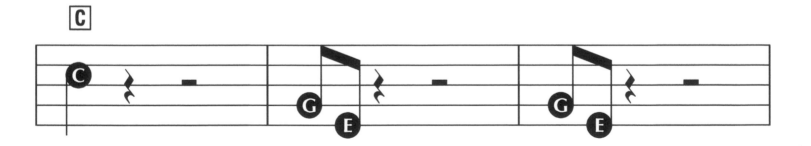

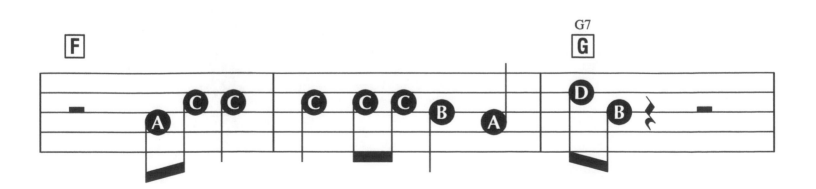

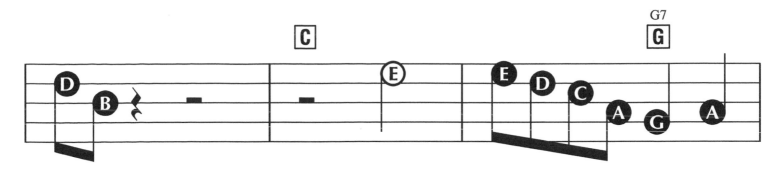

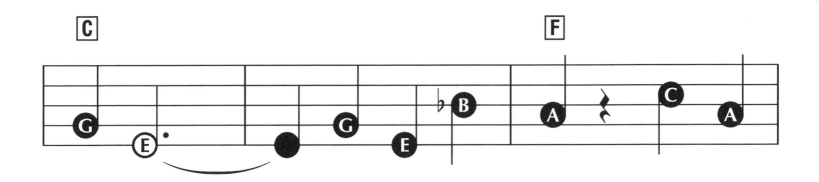

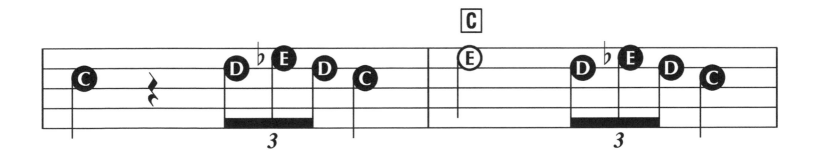

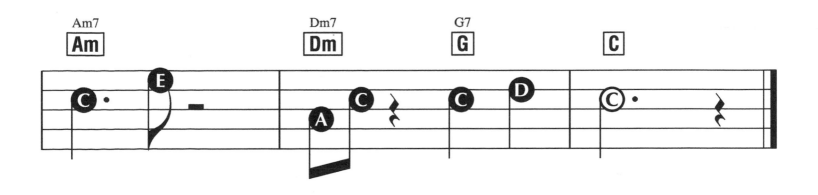

Blue Charlie Brown

Registration 7
Rhythm: Big Band or Swing

By Vince Guaraldi

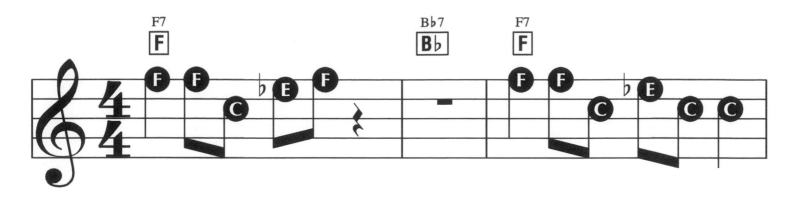

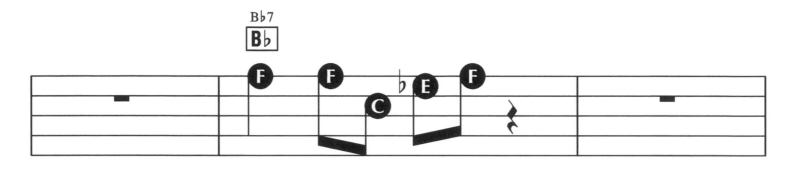

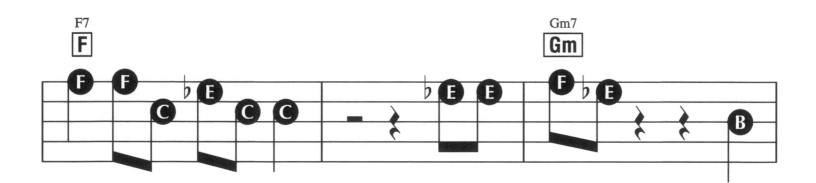

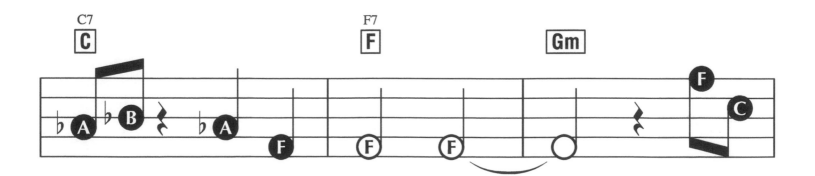

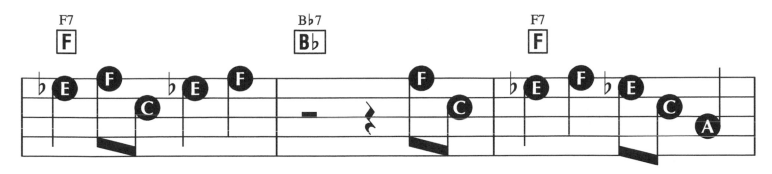

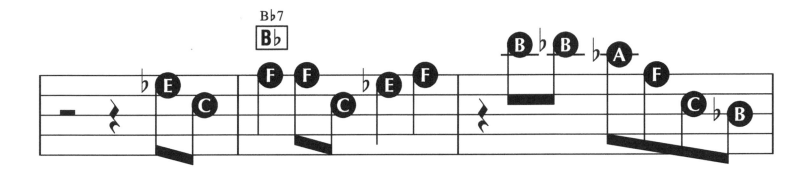

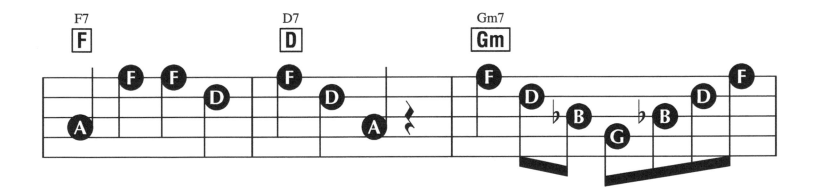

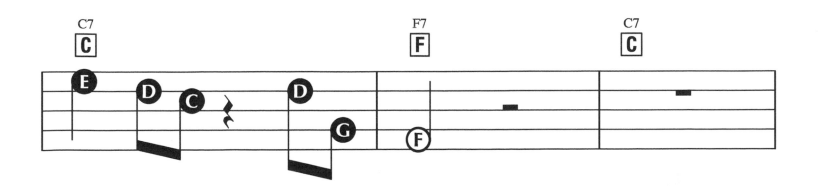

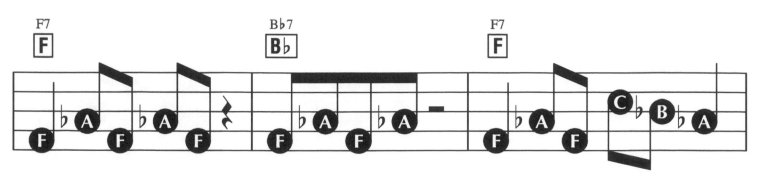

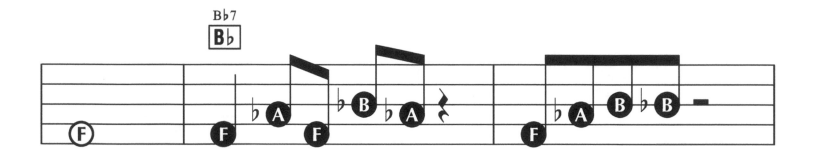

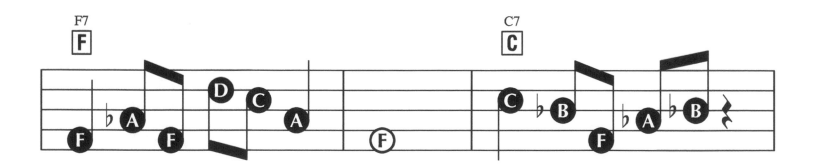

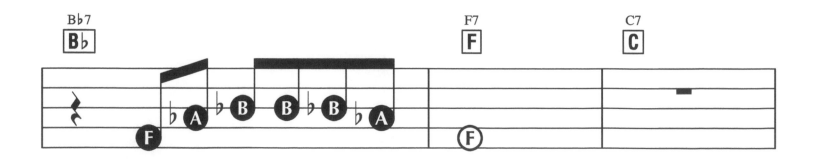

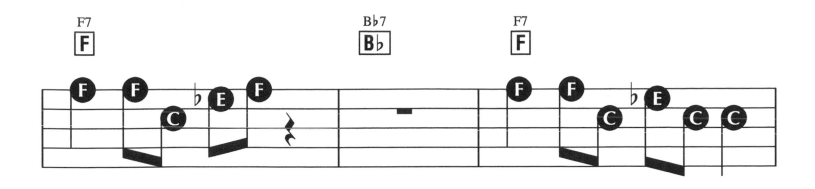

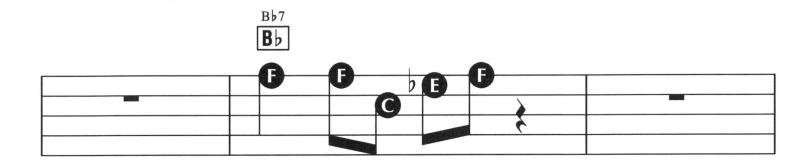

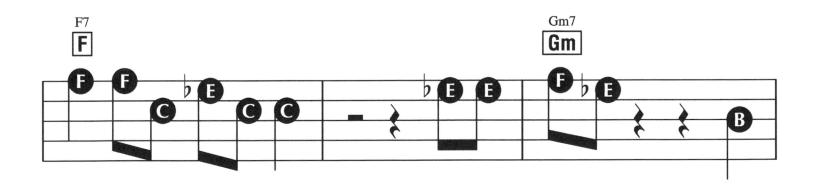

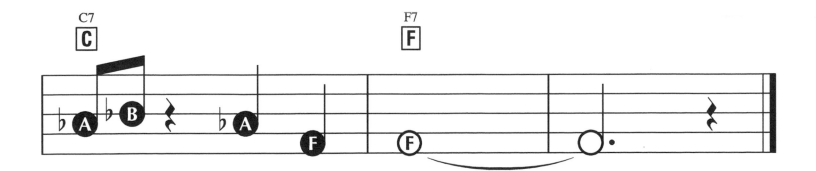

Christmas Time Is Here

Registration 8
Rhythm: Waltz

Words by Lee Mendelson
Music by Vince Guaraldi

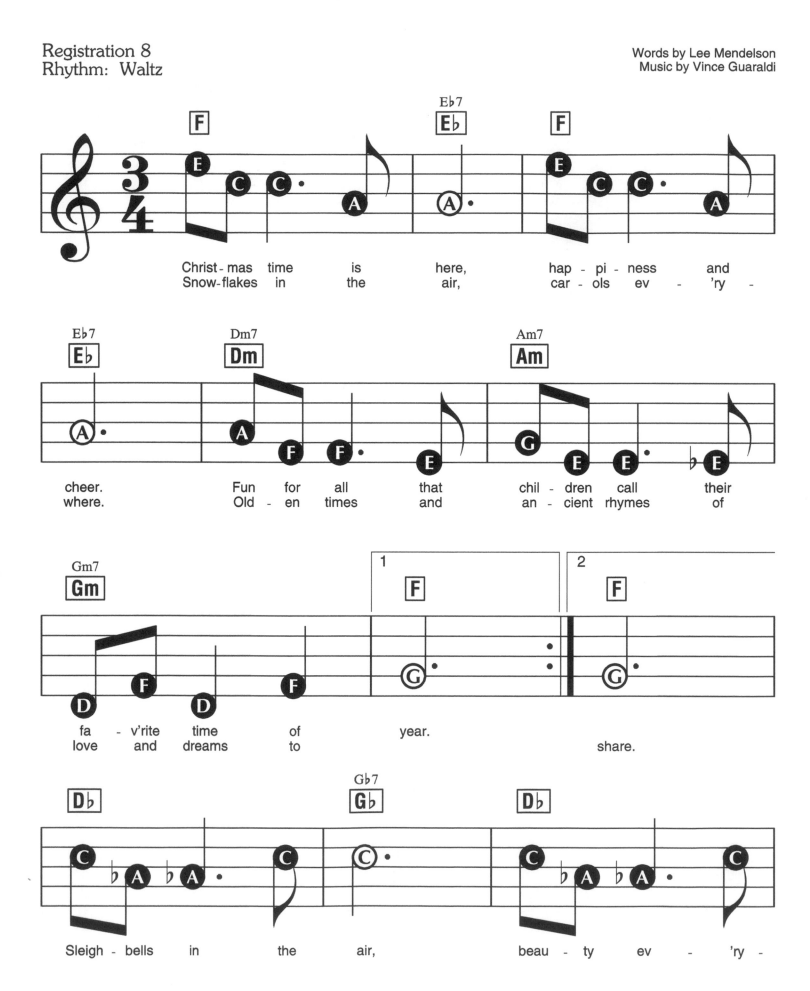

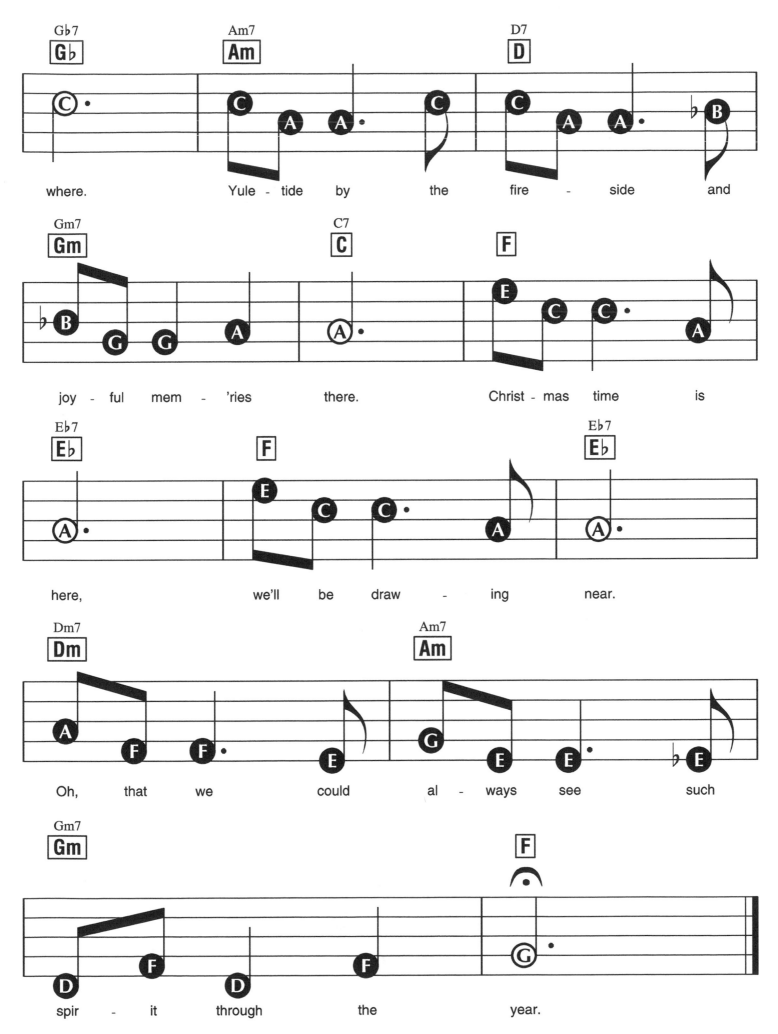

The Great Pumpkin Waltz

Registration 8
Rhythm: Waltz or Jazz Waltz

By Vince Guaraldi

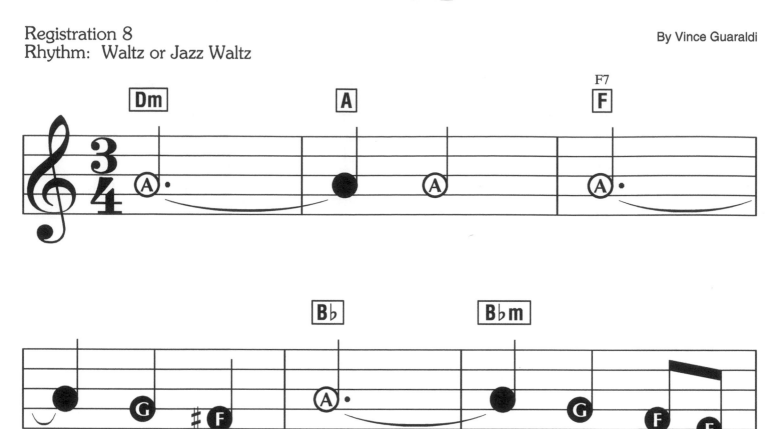

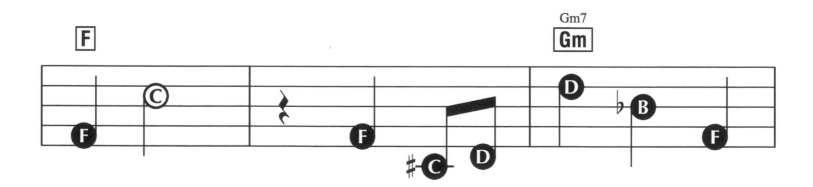

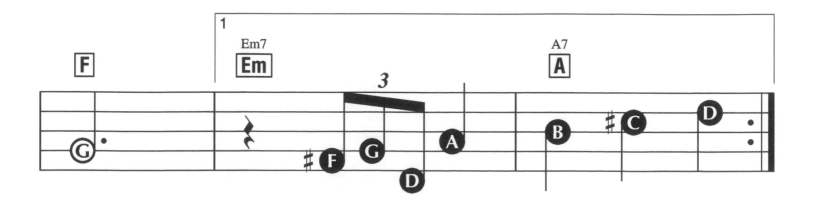

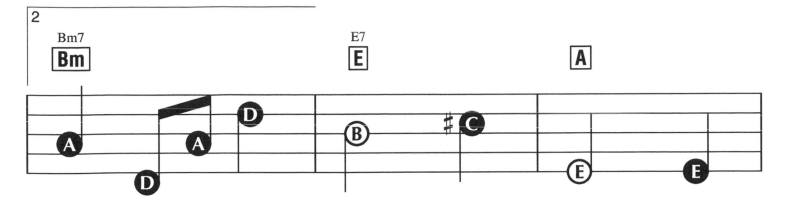

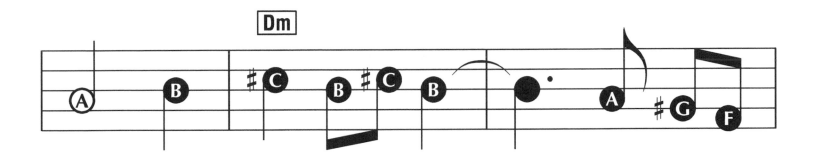

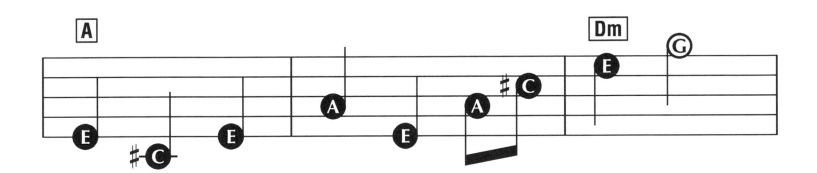

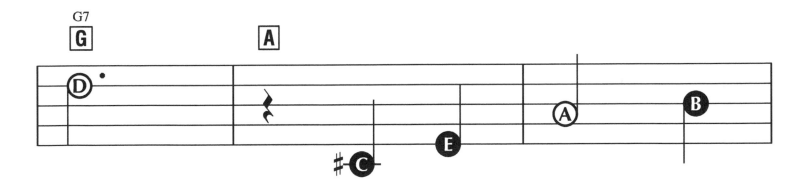

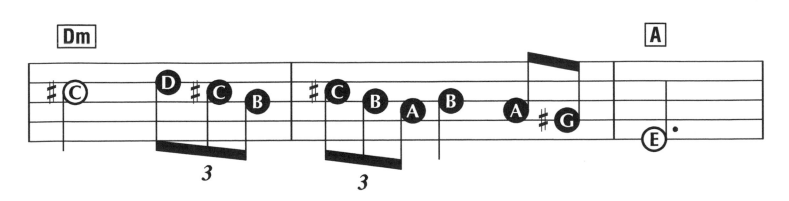

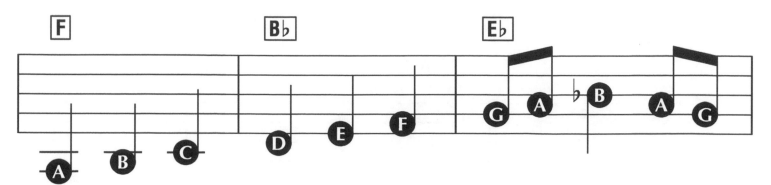

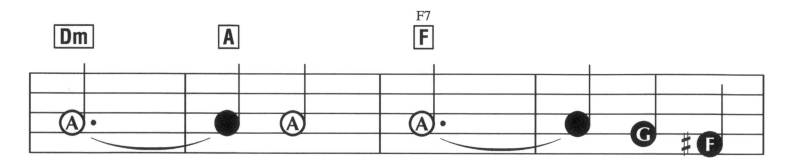

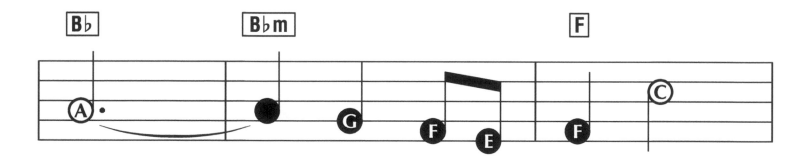

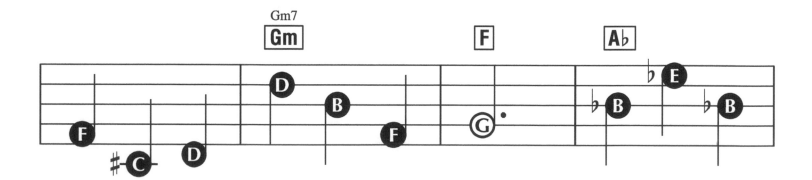

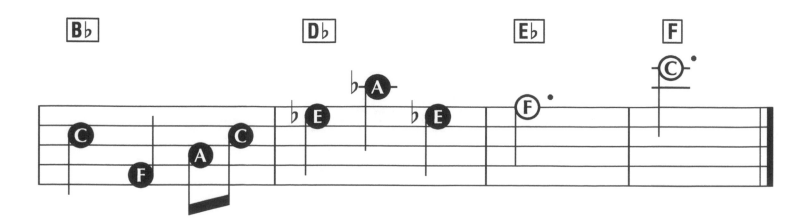

Oh, Good Grief

Registration 8
Rhythm: Bossa Nova or Latin

By Vince Guaraldi

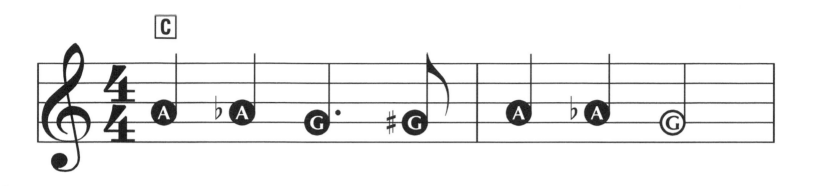

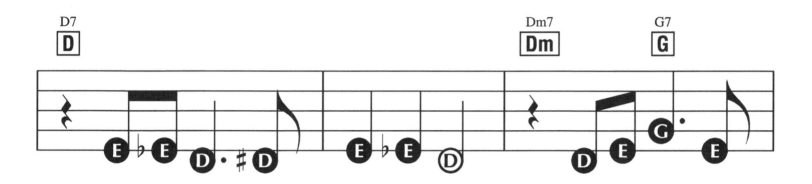

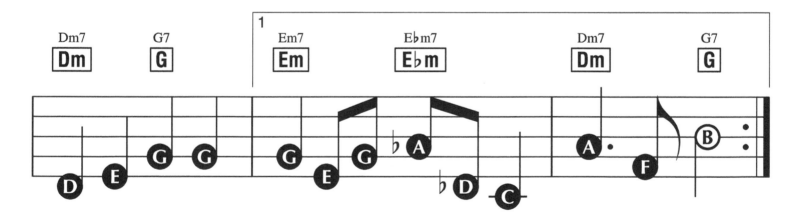

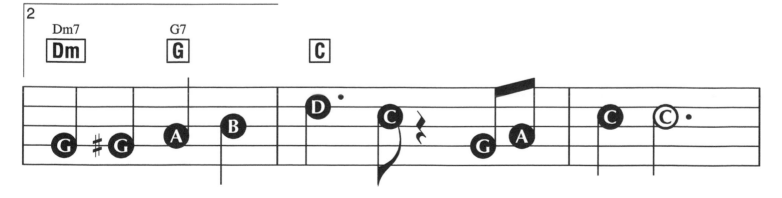

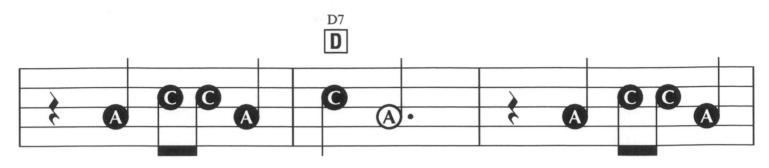

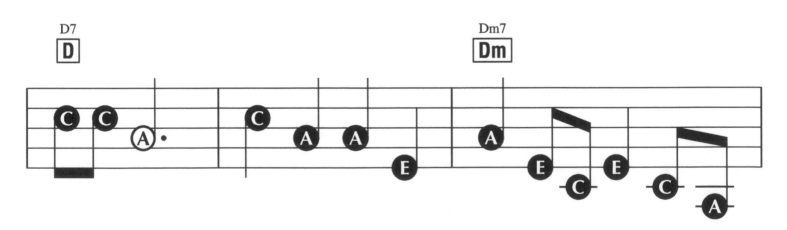

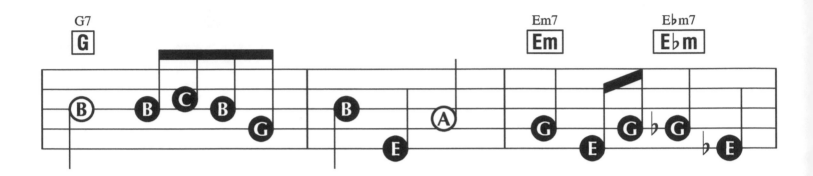

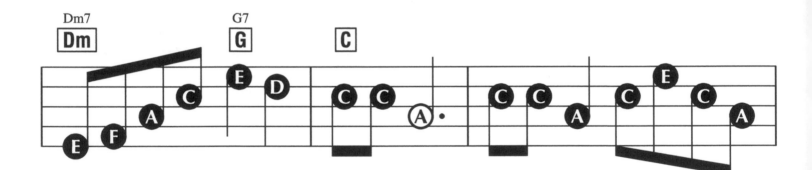

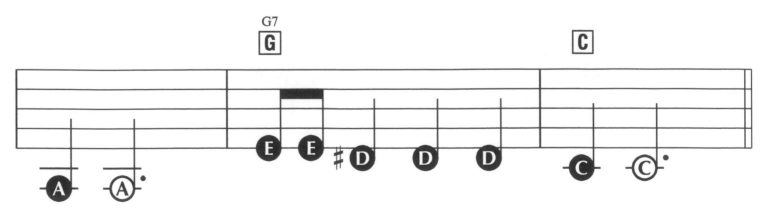

19

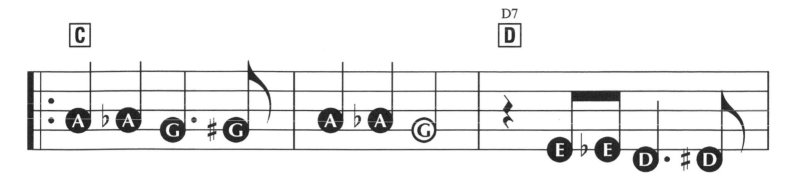

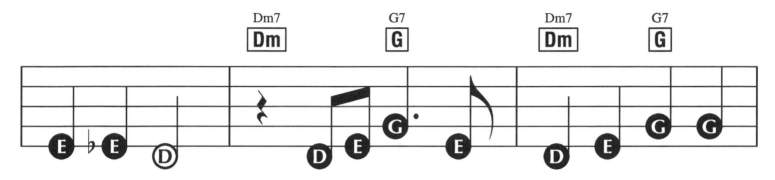

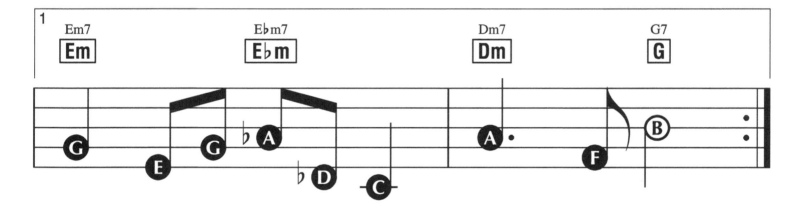

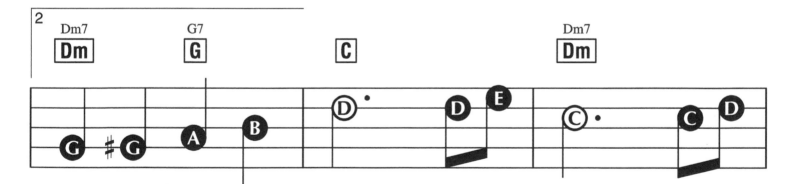

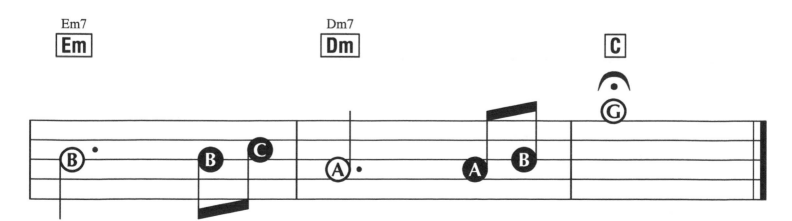

Happiness Theme

Registration 8
Rhythm: Waltz

By Vince Guaraldi

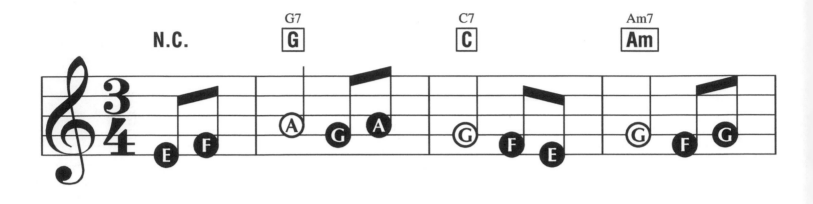

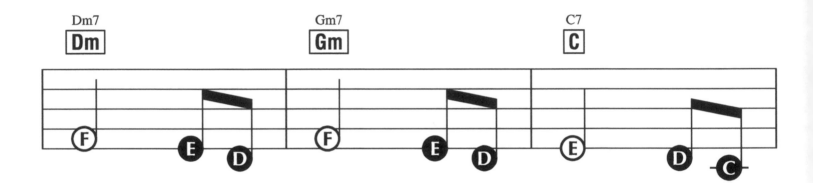

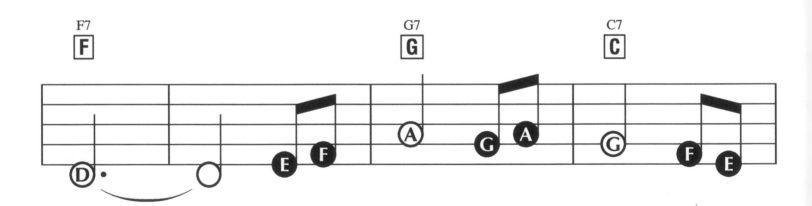

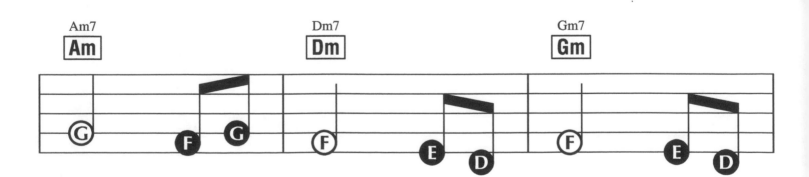

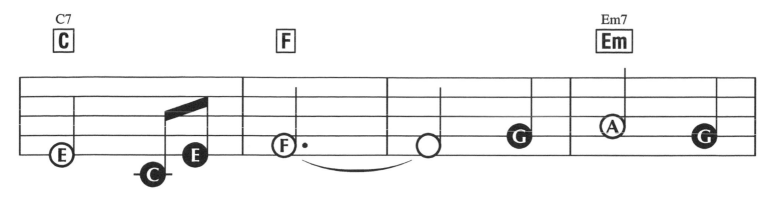

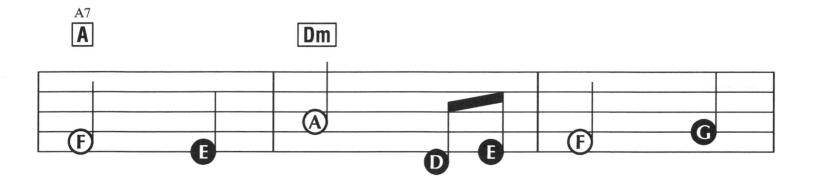

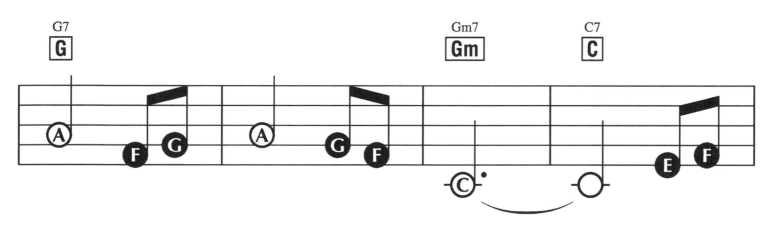

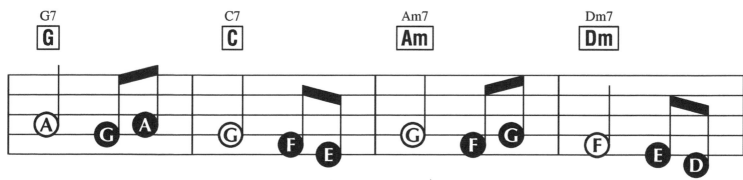

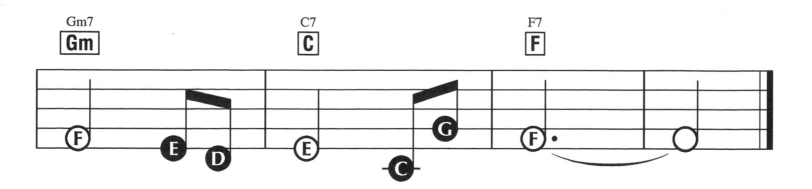

Linus and Lucy

Registration 8
Rhythm: Fox Trot or Swing

By Vince Guaraldi

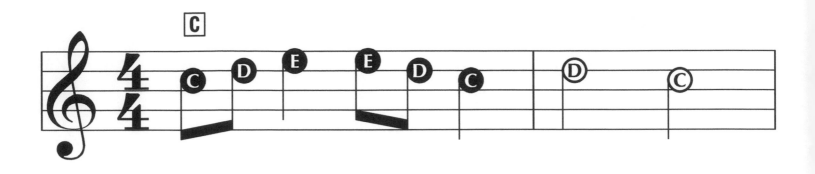

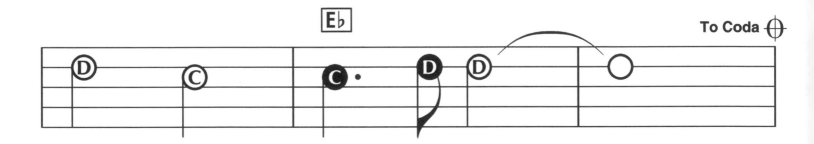

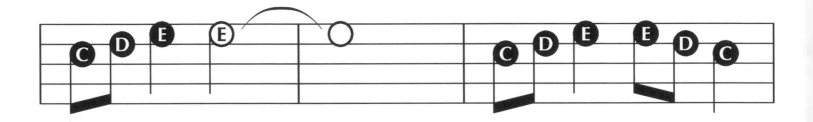

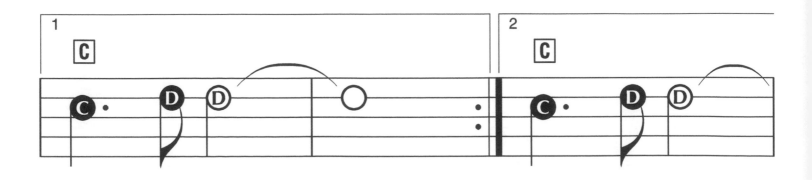

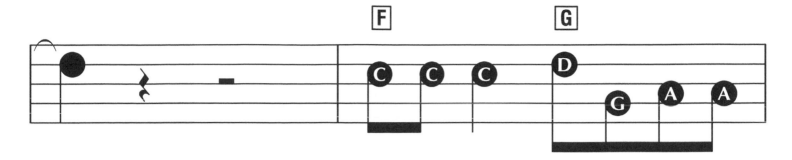

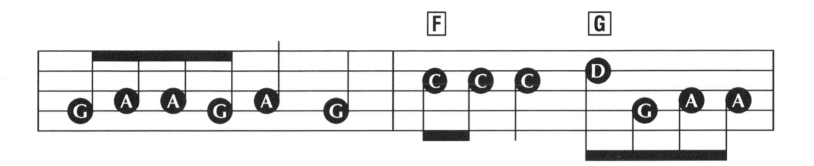

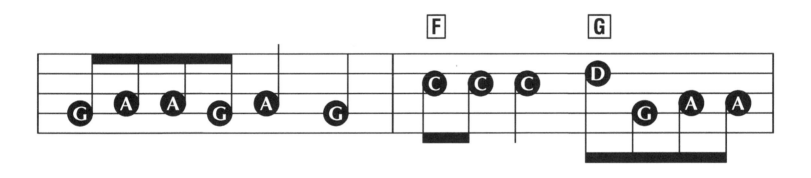

D.C. al Coda
(Return to beginning
Play to ⊕ and
Skip to Coda)

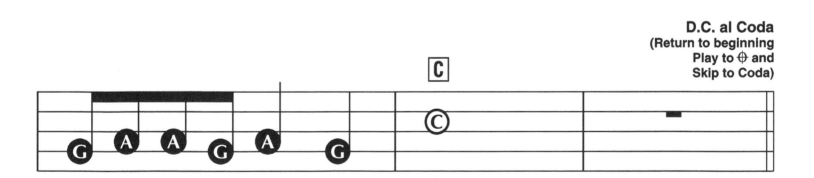

CODA

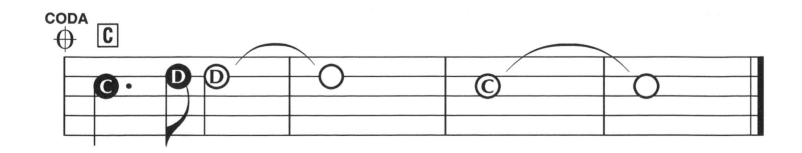

Love Will Come

Registration 3
Rhythm: 4/4 Ballad or Fox Trot

By Vince Guaraldi

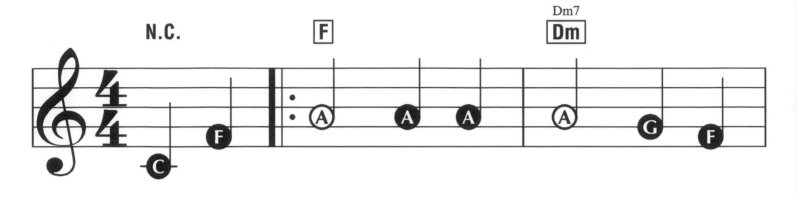

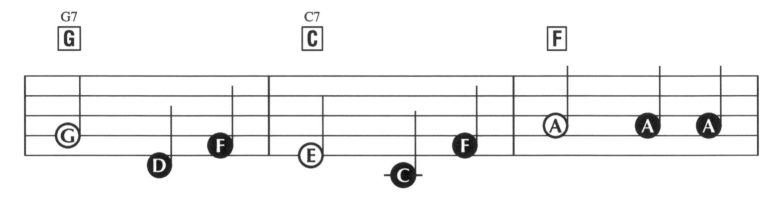

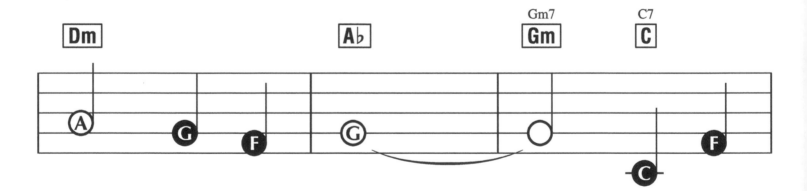

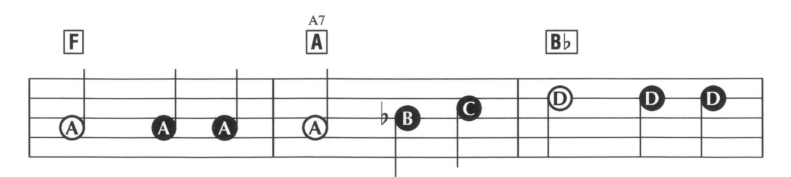

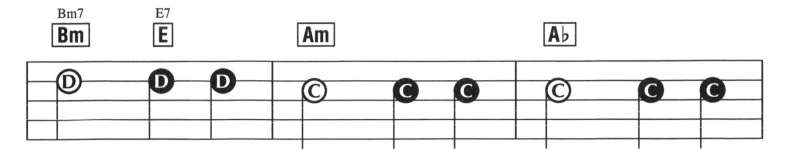

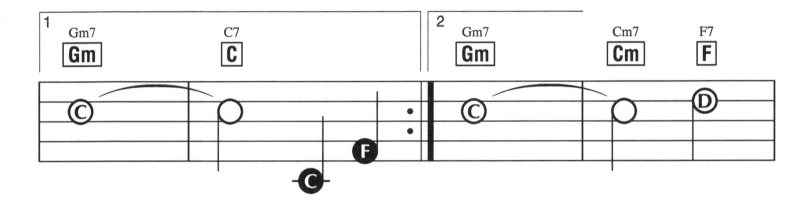

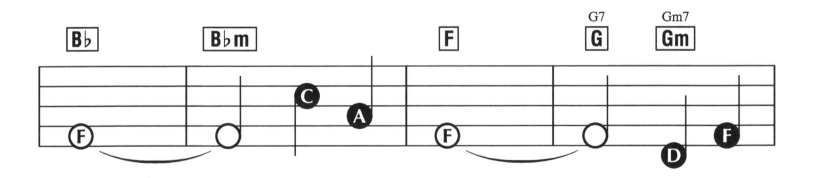

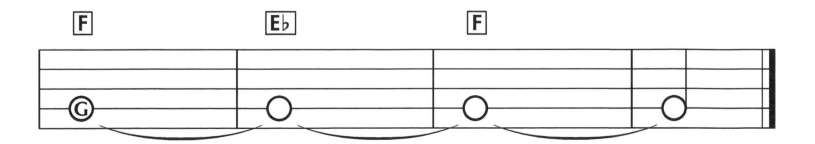

Schroeder

Registration 8
Rhythm: Waltz

By Vince Guaraldi

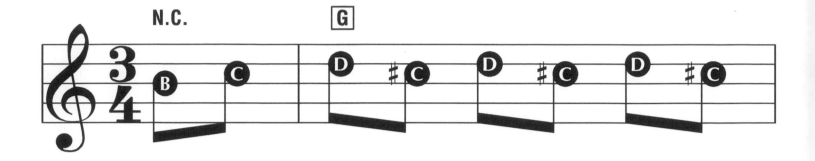

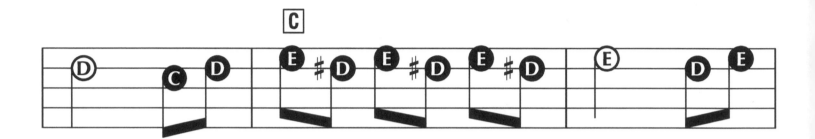

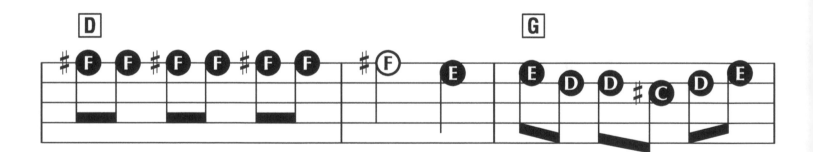

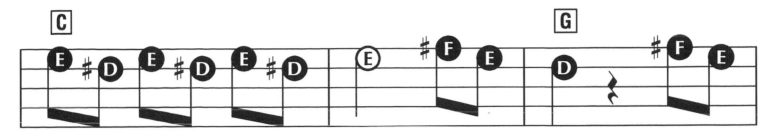

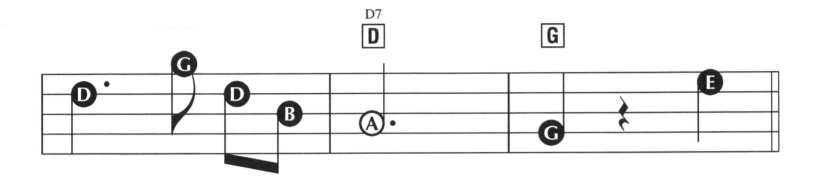

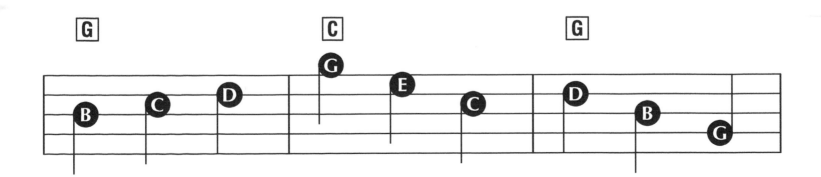

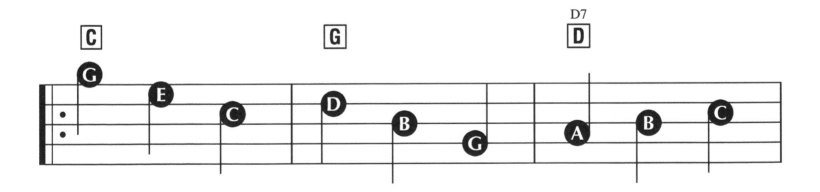

28

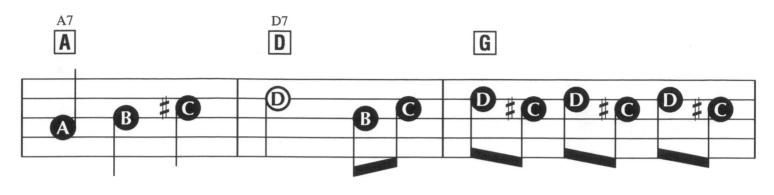

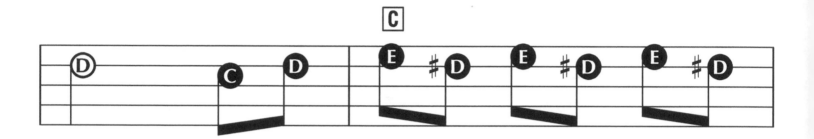

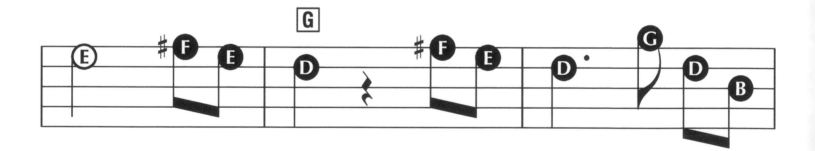

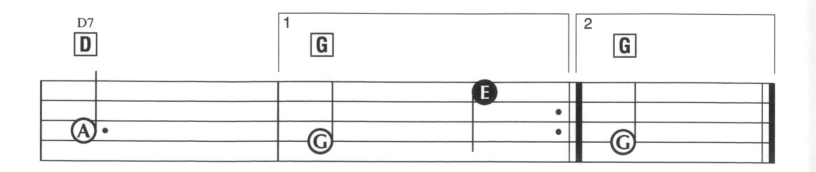

You're in Love, Charlie Brown

Registration 3
Rhythm: Waltz

By Vince Guaraldi

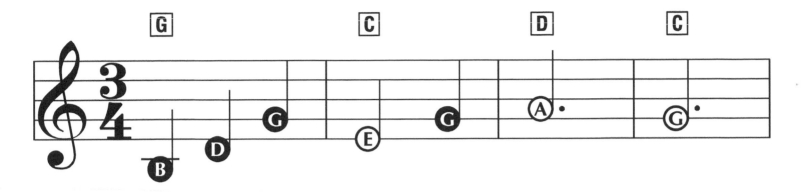

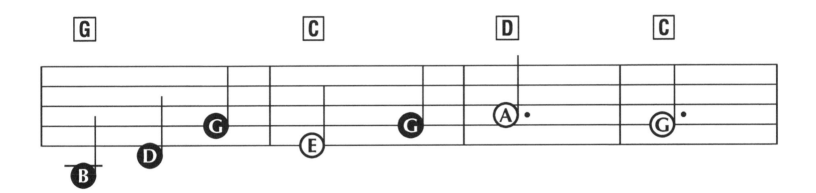

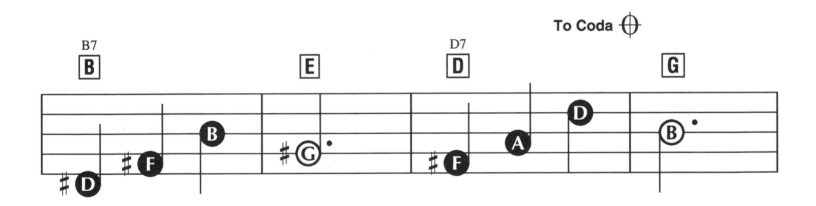

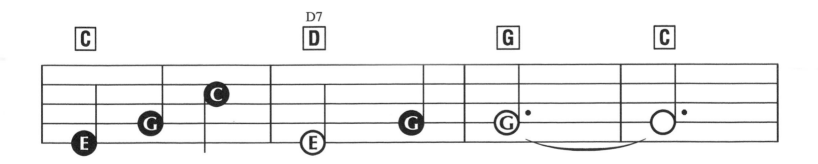

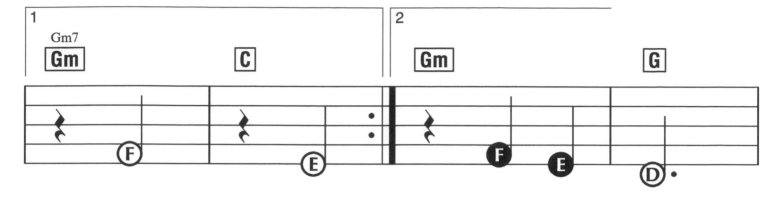

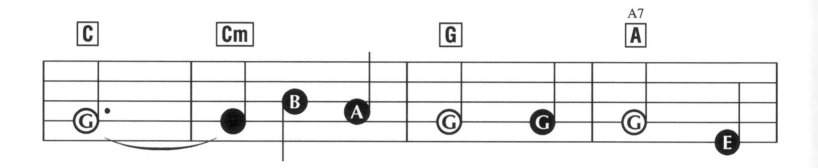

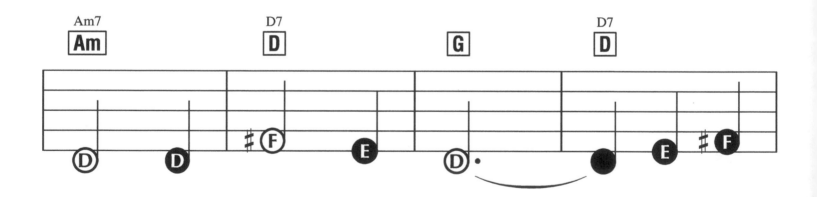

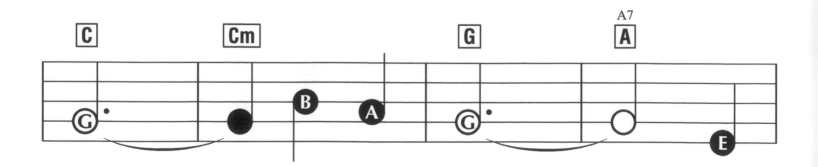

D.C. al Coda
(Return to beginning
Play to ⊕ and
Skip to Coda)

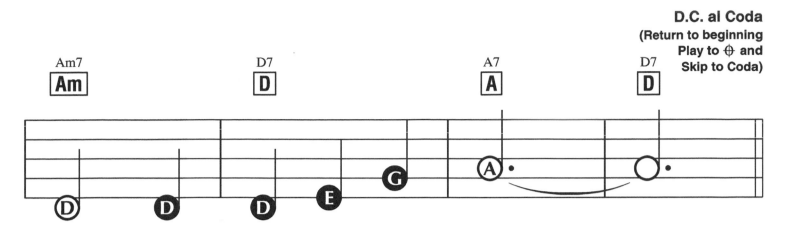

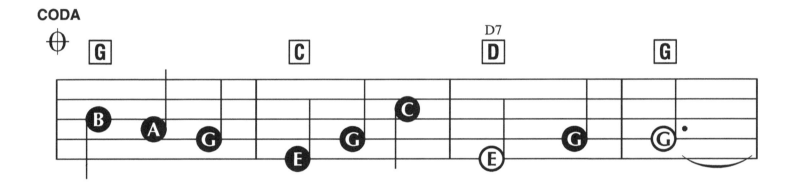

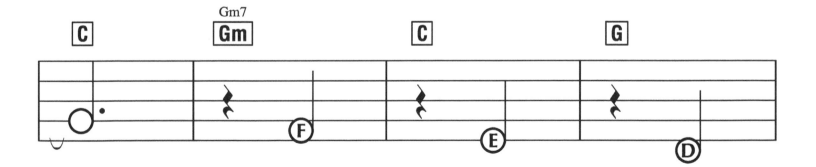

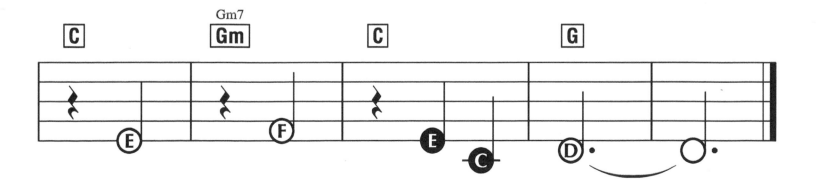

Registration Guide

- Match the Registration number on the song to the corresponding numbered category below. Select and activate an instrumental sound available on your instrument.

- Choose an automatic rhythm appropriate to the mood and style of the song. (Consult your Owner's Guide for proper operation of automatic rhythm features.)

- Adjust the tempo and volume controls to comfortable settings.

Registration

1	Mellow	Flutes, Clarinet, Oboe, Flugel Horn, Trombone, French Horn, Organ Flutes
2	Ensemble	Brass Section, Sax Section, Wind Ensemble, Full Organ, Theater Organ
3	Strings	Violin, Viola, Cello, Fiddle, String Ensemble, Pizzicato, Organ Strings
4	Guitars	Acoustic/Electric Guitars, Banjo, Mandolin, Dulcimer, Ukulele, Hawaiian Guitar
5	Mallets	Vibraphone, Marimba, Xylophone, Steel Drums, Bells, Celesta, Chimes
6	Liturgical	Pipe Organ, Hand Bells, Vocal Ensemble, Choir, Organ Flutes
7	Bright	Saxophones, Trumpet, Mute Trumpet, Synth Leads, Jazz/Gospel Organs
8	Piano	Piano, Electric Piano, Honky Tonk Piano, Harpsichord, Clavi
9	Novelty	Melodic Percussion, Wah Trumpet, Synth, Whistle, Kazoo, Perc. Organ
10	Bellows	Accordion, French Accordion, Mussette, Harmonica, Pump Organ, Bagpipes